THIS WALKER BOOK BELONGS TO:

For Ray with much love V.F.

For Gabriel A.W.

With thanks to Paul Pearce-Kelly,
Head of Invertebrates at London Zoo,
and Alison Pearce-Kelly.

Most spiders are harmless to humans.
There are no poisonous spiders in the British
Isles, but if you live in another country
ask what the dangerous ones look like.

First published 1994
by Walker Books Ltd
87 Vauxhall Walk
London SE11 5HJ

This edition published 1996

2 4 6 8 10 9 7 5 3 1

Text © 1994 Vivian French
Illustrations © 1994 Alison Wisenfeld

This book has been typeset in Bodoni.

Printed in Hong Kong

British Library Cataloguing in Publication Data
A catalogue record for this book is
available from the British Library.

ISBN 0-7445-4735-0

Spider Watching

Written by Vivian French

Illustrated by Alison Wisenfeld

WALKER BOOKS
AND SUBSIDIARIES
LONDON • BOSTON • SYDNEY

House spiders are some of the most common types of spider. Their webs are made from lots of silk threads slung to and fro.

An average house spider won't live much longer than a year, but female Tarantulas can live for more than twenty.

6

My brother loved spiders, and so did I. There were several house spiders living in our shed.

We were very proud of them, so when our cousin Helen came to stay we took her to see them at once.

This is what a spider looks like upside—down through a magnifying glass.

palps —
for tasting, smelling and feeling

bristles —
for sensing things nearby

fangs —
for paralysing prey

spinnerets —
for silk spinning

Spiders are protected by their tough outer skin. But if you pick one up, handle it very carefully.

 *"OOOOOH!"*

She screamed and screamed.
Our mum came running out of the house and
Helen went running in. She said she hated spiders.

"All those hundreds of horrid hairy legs!" she said.

"They've only got eight legs," my brother said,
"and they're not really hairy. It's little bristles.
Do you want to see? You can borrow my
magnifying glass."

But Helen shook her head, and she made us keep
the back door shut.

Spiders belong to a group of animals called "arachnids".

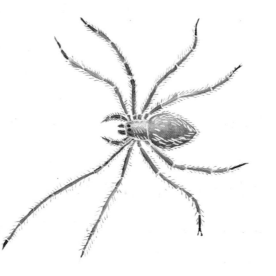

Arachnids have eight legs; insects have six.

Here are a few arachnids:

Scorpion

and

ticks   mites

Harvestman

Tailless whip scorpion

Sun spider

Tailed whip scorpion

We weren't allowed to play in the shed the
next day: we had to go and play in the garden.

"No horrible insects out here," Helen said.

"If you mean spiders," my brother said,
"they're not insects."

My brother liked people to get things right.

The spider has three pairs of spinnerets on the end of its abdomen. It "milks" the silk out with its legs.

The silk is liquid when it comes out, and hardens into a thread in the air.

Spiders are not the only ones who spin thread.

I found a spider's web that sparkled
all over with tiny dew drops.

When you see a spider's web you can be
sure that a spider is hiding nearby.

It sits on one of the lines of the web, waiting for
an insect to land. When it feels the web tremble,
it rushes out to deal with its prey.

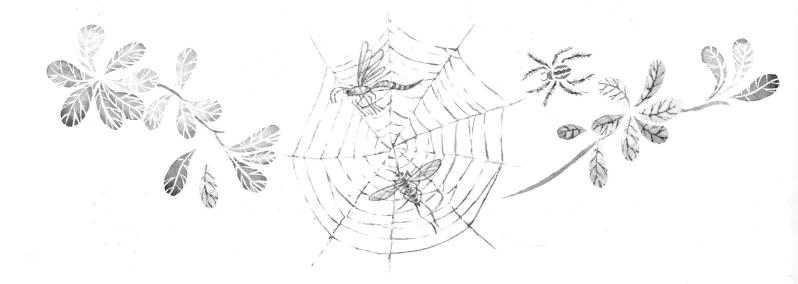

"Come and see!" I said.

Helen came to look.

"It's pretty," she said. "I'm not afraid of webs." She put out her finger to touch it. She only touched it gently, but she tore a big hole in the middle.

"Oh! I didn't mean to!" she said.

"Just watch," said my brother.

Orb Web spider

Ant-mimicking spider

Bolas spider

There are more than thirty thousand different kinds of spider and they all spin silk.

Some spiders, like these, are deadly poisonous and should never be touched.

Northern Black Widow

Red Widow

Sydney Funnel web

A garden spider
came hurrying out from
under a leaf. Helen opened her
mouth to scream, but then she stopped.
The spider ran round the web, and
came up from the bottom to inspect the
hole. She began to swing to and fro,
spinning a thread behind her.

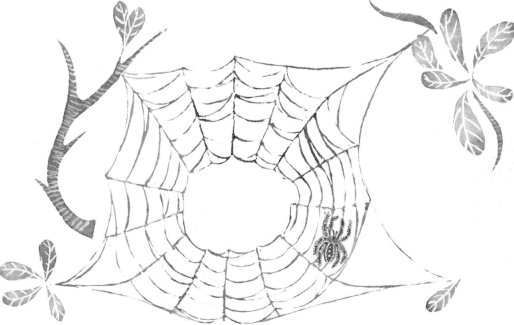

Garden spiders are very common.
This is how they spin their webs.

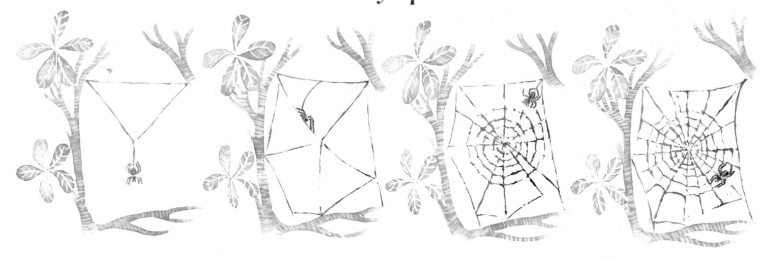

Garden spiders are very neat and tidy. They don't like
holes in their webs and always mend them quickly.

Spiders are not the only ones who mend.

 "Look!" said Helen.
"The hole's all filled in."

My brother snorted. "That's only the working web," he said. He was right. The spider went on spinning until the web was perfect.

"Wow!" said Helen. She was quite close now. "Does the spider ever get it wrong?" My brother looked at her.

"Never," he said.

"That's clever," said Helen.

"Let's have breakfast," I said.

Spiders can only eat liquid food. They stun their prey with their fangs, then inject a special juice into the body. This turns the insides soft enough for the spider to suck out.

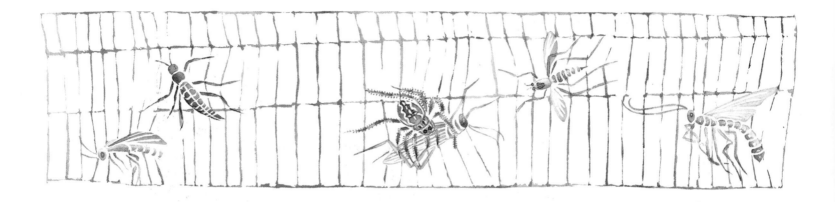

Spiders are not the only

ones who catch their food!

Helen asked about spiders all through breakfast. My brother tried to frighten her by telling her how they suck the juices from flies and other things they catch. Helen wanted to go back and see the spiders in the shed.

"I know where there's a spider's nest," I said.
"Show me!" Helen jumped up.

Spiders are not dirty. House spiders help keep the house clean by catching flies that carry germs. Spiders need water to drink — which is why you often find them in the bath!

Save a spider. . .

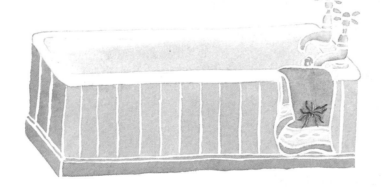

place a towel over the side of the bath.

When we got to the
shed it looked different.
Our mother was there,
and she was brushing
cobwebs off the walls
with a long broom.

"Stop!" My brother and I shouted.

"Please stop!" Helen said.

Our mother looked surprised.
"I thought you hated spiders."

"I like them now," Helen
told her. Our mother
shook her head.

"It was terribly dirty
in here." She picked
up the broom and
went out.

If it senses danger, a spider can run
and hide very quickly. Some spiders
use camouflage to hide themselves.

A spider uses the bristles on its body
and legs to sense movement nearby.

If a spider loses a leg it can grow a new one.

 Helen rubbed her eyes.
"Poor little spiders," she said.
"Are they all dead?"

My brother was peering behind a pile of old paint pots. He waited until our mother had shut the door, and then he grinned. "Look!" he said.

At least seven or eight spiders were already tiptoeing out. They scuttled up into the corners and began to spin their webs.

Female spiders lay their eggs in a sheltered corner and wrap them up in bags of spun silk to keep them safe. There can be hundreds of eggs in each bag.

 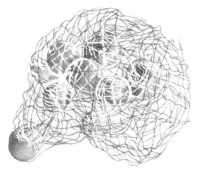 

The nest is fixed firmly in place by sticky silk.

Spider babies are called spiderlings. They hatch out by themselves and then spin a thread to let the wind blow them away from their brothers and sisters.

My brother picked one up.

"Do you want to hold one,
now you like them?"

Helen took a very deep breath.
Then she held out her hand. "All right," she said.

She let the spider walk over her hand and
she only made a very little squeak.

"You squealed!" my brother said,
putting the spider back.

"Only because I remembered
about the nest," Helen said.
"Can I see it now?"

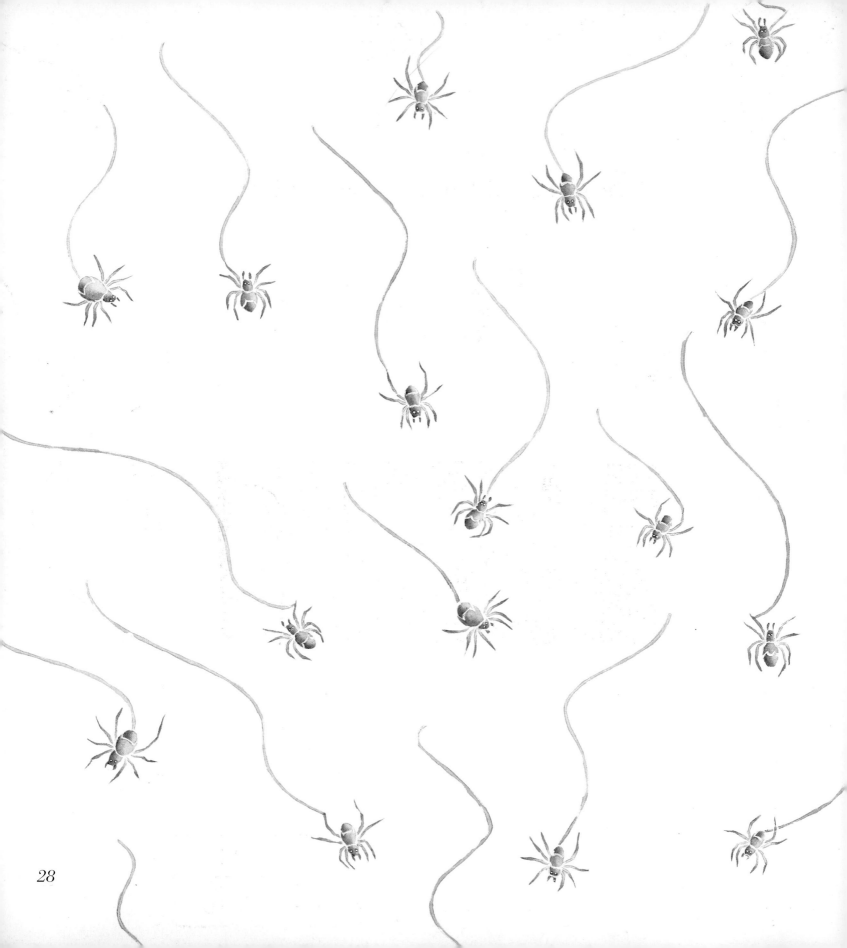

28

So I showed her, and she loved it.

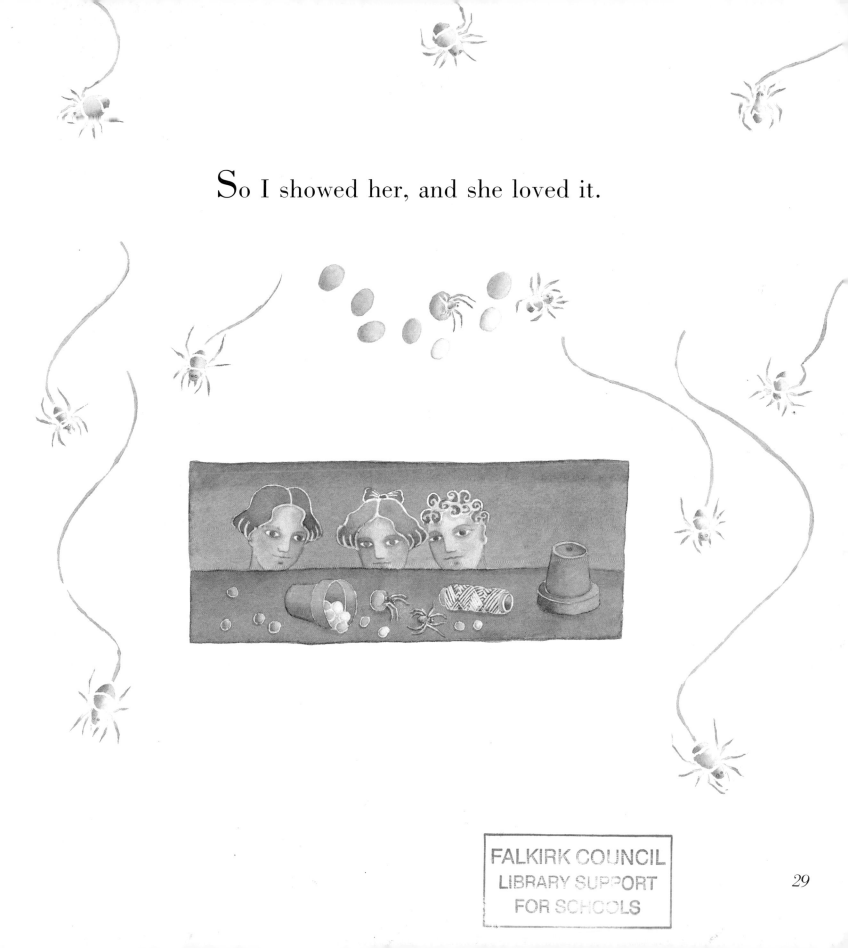

29

INDEX

Look up the pages to find out
about all these spidery things.
Don't forget to look at both
kinds of words: this kind
and this kind.

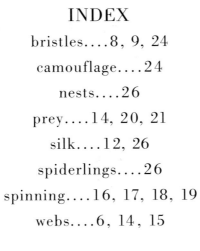

MORE WALKER PAPERBACKS
For You to Enjoy

Read and Wonder

"These books fulfil all the requirements of a factual picture book,
but also supply that imaginative element." *The Independent on Sunday*

THE APPLE TREES
Vivian French/Terry Milne

"A highly individual look at an aspect of the world showing
non-fiction can be as engaging as story… The illustrations are beautiful."
The School Librarian

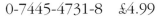

0-7445-4731-8   £4.99

CATERPILLAR CATERPILLAR
by Vivian French/Charlotte Voake

Shortlisted for the Kurt Maschler Award

"Charming and very informative … good natural history." *Books for Keeps*

0-7445-3636-7   £4.99

THINK OF AN EEL
by Karen Wallace/Mike Bostock

Winner of the Times Educational Supplement's
Junior Information Book Award and the Kurt Maschler Award

"Simply stunning… An extraordinarily impressive book…
Beautifully written … superb illustrations." *Children's Books of the Year*

0-7445-3639-1   £4.99

Walker Paperbacks are available from most booksellers, or by post from B.B.C.S., P.O. Box 941, Hull, North Humberside HU1 3YQ

24 hour telephone credit card line 01482 224626

To order, send: Title, author, ISBN number and price for each book ordered, your full name and address,
cheque or postal order payable to BBCS for the total amount and allow the following for postage and packing:
UK and BFPO: £1.00 for the first book, and 50p for each additional book to a maximum of £3.50.
Overseas and Eire: £2.00 for the first book, £1.00 for the second and 50p for each additional book.

Prices and availability are subject to change without notice.